HESED

GOD'S LOVE
AND
KINDNESS

CHARLES TABRON

Hesed: God's Love and Kindness

Trilogy Christian Publishers A Wholly Owned Subsidiary of Trinity Broadcasting Network

2442 Michelle Drive Tustin, CA 92780

Trilogy Christian Publishing/TBN and colophon are trademarks of Trinity Broadcasting Network.

Cover design by: __

For information about special discounts for bulk purchases, please contact Trilogy Christian Publishing.

Trilogy Disclaimer: The views and content expressed in this book are those of the author and may not necessarily reflect the views and doctrine of Trilogy Christian Publishing or the Trinity Broadcasting Network.

Manufactured in the United States of America

10 9 8 7 6 5 4 3 2 1

Library of Congress Cataloging-in-Publication Data is available.

ISBN: 978-1-63769-874-7

E-ISBN: 978-1-63769-875-4

INTRODUCTION PRAYER

Heavenly Father, I humble myself before you. Thank you for hearing me. Allow *Hesed* to show humanity your infinite love and kindness. May they see your abundant *Hesed* through Christ Jesus, your only begotten Son. You, Heavenly Father, are Omnipresent, being anywhere and everywhere at once. Send *Hesed* with your Word to people and places around the world. For you, Father God, are Omnipotent, having unlimited power to do anything because all things are yours. Let *Hesed* with your Word enter the hearts of humanity. Holy One, you are Omniscient, having complete unlimited knowledge, awareness, and understanding perceiving all things. Nothing escapes your *Hesed* and your Word. Lord, you are Omnibenevolent, possessing perfect and unlimited goodness. Shower unbelievers with your *Hesed* to inspire them to believe and worship you. May they receive the inheritance of salvation.

To God be the Glory. Amen.

CONTENT

God Loves You

For God so loved the world that He gave His only begotten Son, that whosoever believes in Him should not perish but have everlasting life. For God did not send His Son into the world to condemn the world, but that the world through Him might be saved.

John 3:16, 17 (NKJV)

If you confess with your mouth the Lord Jesus and believe in your heart that God has raised Him from the dead, you will be saved. For with the heart one believes unto righteousness, and with the mouth confession is made unto salvation. For the Scripture says, "Whosoever believes on Him will not be put to shame.

Romans 10:9–11 (NKJV)

For He made Him who knew no sin to be sin for us, that we might become the righteousness of God in Him.

2 Corinthians 5:21 (NKJV)

For by grace, you have been saved through faith, and that not of yourselves; it is the gift of God, not of works, lest anyone should boast. For we are His workmanship, created in Christ Jesus for good works, which God prepared beforehand that we should walk in them.

Ephesians 2:8–10 (NKJV)

*For you were brought at a price; therefore glorify
God in your body [1] and in your spirit, which are
God's.*

1 Corinthians 6:20 (NKJV)

*For the law of the Spirit of life in Christ Jesus has
made me free from the law of sin and death.*

Romans 8:2 (NKJV)

*Now you are the body of Christ, and members
individually.*

1 Corinthians 12:27 (NKJV)

*All praise to God, the Father of our Lord Jesus,
who has blessed us with every spiritual blessing
in the heavenly realms because we are united with
Christ. Even before he made the world, God loved
us and chose us in Christ to be holy and without
fault in his eyes. God decided in advance to adopt
us into his own family by bringing us to himself
through Jesus Christ. This is what he wanted to
do, and it gave him great pleasure. So we praise
God for the glorious grace he has poured out on
us [2] who belong to his dear Son.*

Ephesians 1:3–6 (NLT)

The Word of God

In the beginning was the Word, and the Word was with God, and the Word was God.

John 1:1 (NKJV)

And the Word became flesh and dwelt among us, and we beheld His glory, the glory as of the only begotten of the Father, full of grace and truth.

John 1:14 (NKJV)

Most assuredly, I say to you, he who hears My word and believes in Him who sent Me has everlasting life, and shall not come into judgment, but has passed from death into life.

John 5:24 (NKJV)

All Scripture is given by inspiration of God, and is profitable for doctrine, for reproof, for correction, for instruction in righteousness, that the man of God may be complete, thoroughly equipped for every good work.

2 Timothy 3:16, 17 (NKJV)

For the word of God is living and powerful, and sharper than any two-edged sword, piercing even to the division of soul and spirit, and of joints and marrow, and is a discerner of the thoughts and intents of the heart.
And there is no creature hidden from His sight, but all things are naked and open to the eyes of Him to whom we must give account.

Hebrews 4:12, 13 (NKJV)

So shall My word be that goes forth from My mouth;
It shall not return to Me void,[3]
But it shall accomplish what I please,
And it shall prosper in the thing for which I sent it.

Isaiah 55:11 (NKJV)

Be diligent to present yourself approved to God, a worker who does not need to be ashamed, rightly dividing the word of truth. But shun profane and idle babblings, for they will increase to more ungodliness.

2 Timothy 2:15, 16 (NKJV)

But be doers of the word, and not hearers only deceiving yourselves.

James 1:22 (NKJV)

But He said, "More than that, blessed are those who hear the word of God and keep it!"

Luke 11:28 (NKJV)

So, then faith comes by hearing, and hearing by the word of God.

Romans 10:17 (NKJV)

And take the helmet of salvation, and the sword of the Spirit, which is the word of God.

Ephesians 6:17 (NKJV)

For the word of the Lord is right,
and all His work is done in truth . . .
By the word of the Lord the heavens were made,
And all the host of them by the breath of His
mouth.

Psalm 33:4–6 (NKJV)

Who Is God

God said to Moses, "I AM WHO I AM." And He said, "Thus you shall say to the children of Israel, 'I AM has sent me to you.'"

Exodus 3:14 (NKJV)

I am the Alpha and Omega, the Beginning and the End, the First and the Last.[4]

Revelation 22:13 (NKJV)

God is Spirit, and those who worship Him must worship in spirit and truth.

John 4:24 (NKJV)

For by Him all things were created that are in heaven and on earth, visible and invisible, whether thrones or dominion or [5]*principalities or* [6]*powers.*
All things were created through Him and for Him. And He is before all things, and in Him all things consist.

Colossians 1:16, 17 (NKJV)

The Lord by wisdom founded the earth;
By understanding He established the heavens;
By His knowledge the depths were broken up,
And clouds drop down the dew.

Proverbs 3:19, 20 (NKJV)

For every beast of the forest is Mine,
And the cattle on a thousand hills.
I know all the birds of the mountains,
And the wild beasts of the field are Mine.
If I were hungry, I would not tell you;

19

For the world is Mine, and all its fullness.

Psalm 50:10–12 (NKJV)

For the Lord your God is a merciful God, He will not forsake you nor destroy you, nor forget the covenant of your fathers which He swore to them.

Deuteronomy 4:31 (NKJV)

Therefore, know that the Lord your God, He is God, the faithful God who keeps covenant and mercy for a thousand generations with those who love Him and keep His commandments.

Deuteronomy 7:9 (NKJV)

He who does not love does not know God, for God is love.

1 John 4:8 (NKJV)

In this the love of God was manifested toward us, that God has sent His only begotten Son into the world, that we might live through Him.

1 John 4:9 (NKJV)

In this is love, not that we loved God, but that He loved us and sent His Son to be the propitiation for our sins.

1 John 4:10 (NKJV)

Beloved, if God so loved us, we also ought to love one another.

1 John 4:11 (NKJV)

Know Who
You Are

Then God said, "Let Us make man in Our image, according to Our likeness; let them have dominion over the fish of sea, over the birds of the air, and over the cattle, over [7]all the earth and over every creeping thing that creeps on the earth."

Genesis 1:26 (NKJV)

So God created man in His own image, in the image of God He created him; male and female He created them.

Genesis 1:27 (NKJV)

And the Lord God formed man of the dust of the ground, and breathed into his nostrils the breath of life; and man became a living being.

Genesis 2:7 (NKJV)

I said, "You are [8]gods,
And all of you are children of the Most High."

Psalm 82:6 (NKJV)

For all who are led by the Spirit of God are sons of God.

Romans 8:14 (AMPC)

For you did not receive the spirit of bondage again to fear, but you received the Spirit of adoption by whom we cry out "Abba, Father."

Romans 8:15 (NKJV)

The Spirit Himself bears witness with our spirit that we are children of God, and if children, then heirs—heirs of God and joint heirs with Christ, if

23

indeed we suffer with Him, that we may also be glorified together.

Romans 8:16, 17 (NKJV)

However, the spiritual is not first, but the natural, and afterward the spiritual. The first man was of the earth, made[9] of dust; the second Man is[10] the Lord from heaven.

1 Corinthians 15:46, 47 (NKJV)

As was the man of dust, so also are those who are made of dust; and as is the heavenly Man, so also are those who are heavenly. And as we have borne the image of the man of dust, we shall also bear[11] the image of the heavenly Man.

1 Corinthians 15:48, 49 (NKJV)

And if you are Christ's, then you are Abraham's seed, and heirs according to the promise.

Galatians 3:29 (NKJV)

...and from Jesus Christ, the faithful witness, the firstborn from the dead, and the ruler over the kings of the earth. To Him who [12]loved us and washed us from our sins in His own blood.

Revelation 1:5 (NKJV)

...and has made us [13]kings and priests to His God and Father, to Him be glory and dominion forever and ever. Amen.

Revelation 1:6 (NKJV)

Know Your Authority

And Jesus came and spoke to them, saying, "All authority has been given to Me in heaven and on earth."

Matthew 28:18 (NKJV)

Behold, I give you the authority to trample on serpents and scorpions, and over all the power of the enemy, and nothing shall by any means hurt you.

Luke 10:19 (NKJV)

So Jesus answered and said to them, "Have faith in God. For assuredly, I say to you, whoever says to this mountain, 'Be removed and be cast into the sea,' and does not doubt in his heart, but believes that those things he says will be done, he will have whatever he says."

Mark 11:22, 23 (NKJV)

Therefore, I say to you, whatever things you ask when you pray, believe that you receive them, and you will have them.

Mark 11:24 (NKJV)

Most assuredly, I say to you, he who believes in Me, the works that I do he will do also; and greater works than these he will do, because I go to My Father.

John 14:12 (NKJV)

And whatever you ask in My name, that I will do, that the Father may be glorified in the Son.

John 14:13 (NKJV)

27

If you ¹⁴ask anything in My name, I will do it.

John 14:14 (NKJV)

For the grace of God that brings salvation has appeared to all men, teaching us that, denying ungodliness and worldly lust, we should live soberly, righteously, and godly in this present age, looking for the blessed hope and glorious appearing of our great God and Savior Jesus Christ, who gave Himself for us, that He might redeem us from every lawless deed and purify for Himself His own special people, zealous for good works.

Speak these things, exhort, and rebuke with all authority. Let no one despise you.

Titus 2:11–15 (NKJV)

Sin

Jesus was led up by the Spirit into the wilderness to be tempted by the devil. And when He had fasted forty days and forty nights, afterward He was hungry.

Now when the tempter came to Him, he said, "If You are the Son of God, command that these stones become bread."

But He answered and said, "It is written, 'Man shall not live by bread alone, but by every word that proceeds from the mouth of God.'"

Matthew 4:1–4 (NKJV)

Then the devil took Him up into the holy city, set Him on the pinnacle of the temple, and said to Him, "If You are the Son of God, throw Yourself down. For it is written: 'He shall give His angels charge over you,' and, 'In their hands they shall bear you up, lest you dash your foot against a stone.'" Jesus said to him, "It is written again, 'You shall not tempt the Lord your God.'"

Matthew 4:5–7 (NKJV)

Again, the devil took Him up on an exceeding high mountain, and showed Him all the kingdoms of the world and their glory. And he said to Him, "All these things I will give to You if You will fall down and worship me."

Then Jesus said to him,[15] "Away with you, Satan! For it is written, 'You shall worship the Lord your God, and Him only you shall serve.'"

Matthew 4:8–10 (NKJV)

Then the devil left Him, and behold, angels came and ministered to Him.

Matthew 4:11 (NKJV)

For we do not have a High Priest who cannot sympathize with our weaknesses, but was in all points tempted as we are, yet without sin.

Hebrews 4:15 (NKJV)

Do not love the world or the things in the world. If anyone loves the world, the love of the Father is not in him. For all that is in the world—the lust of the flesh, the lust of the eyes, and the pride of life—is not of the Father but is of the world. And the world is passing away, and the lust of it; but he who does the will of God abides forever.

1 John 2:15–17 (NKJV)

Set your mind on things above, not on things on the earth . . . Therefore, put to death your members which are on the earth: fornication, uncleanness, passion, evil desire, and covetousness, which is idolatry. Because of these things the wrath of God is coming upon the sons of disobedience, in which you yourselves once walked when you lived in them.

Colossians 3:2–7 (NKJV)

But now you yourselves are to put off all these: anger, wrath, malice, blasphemy, filthy language out of your mouth. Do not lie to one another, since you have put off the old man with his deeds, and have put on the new man who is renewed in knowledge according to the image of Him who created him.

Colossians 3:8–10 (NKJV)

For the wages of sin is death, but the ¹⁶gift of God is eternal life in Christ Jesus our Lord.

Romans 6:23 (NKJV)

Therefore, to him who knows to do good and does not do it, to him it is sin.

James 4:17 (NKJV)

Repentance

Draw near to God and He will draw near to you. Cleanse your hands, you sinners; and purify your hearts, you double-minded . . . Humble yourselves in the sight of the Lord, and He will lift you up.

James 4:8–10 (NKJV)

Then I will give them a heart to know Me, that I am the Lord, and they shall be My people, and I will be their God, for they shall return to Me with their whole heart.

Jeremiah 24:7 (NKJV)

If My people who are called by My name will humble themselves, and pray and seek My face, and turn from their wicked ways, then I will hear from heaven, and will forgive their sin and heal their land.

2 Chronicles 7:14 (NKJV)

I have not come to call the righteous, but sinners, to repentance.

Luke 5:32 (NKJV)

From that time Jesus began to preach and say, "Repent, for the kingdom of heaven [17] is at hand."

Matthew 4:17 (NKJV)

Truly, these times of ignorance God overlooked, but now commands all men everywhere to repent.

Acts 17:30 (NKJV)

Remember therefore how you have received and heard; hold fast and repent. Therefore, if you will not watch, I will come upon you as a thief, and you will not know what hour I will come upon you.

Revelation 3:3 (NKJV)

The soul who sins shall die. The son shall not bear the guilt of the father, nor the father bear the guilt of the son. The righteousness of the righteous shall be upon himself, and the wickedness of the wicked shall be upon himself. "...For I have no pleasure in the death of one who dies," says the Lord. "Therefore, turn and live!"

Ezekiel 18:20, 32 (NKJV)

Likewise, I say to you, there is joy in the presence of the angels of God over one sinner who repents.

Luke 15:10 (NKJV)

Jesus Christ the Savior

I am the door. If anyone enters by Me, he will be saved, and will go out and find pasture.

John 10:9 (NKJV)

The thief does not come except to steal and to kill, and to destroy. I have come that they may have life, and that they may have it more abundantly.

John 10:10 (NKJV)

And it shall come to pass,
That whoever calls on the name of the Lord
Shall be [18]saved. For in Mount Zion and in Jerusalem there shall be [19]deliverance, As the Lord has said, Among the remnant whom the Lord calls.

Joel 2:32 (NKJV)

If you confess with your mouth the Lord Jesus and believe in your heart that God has raised Him from the dead, you will be saved.

Romans 10:9 (NKJV)

For with the heart one believes unto righteousness, and with the mouth confession is made unto salvation.

Romans 10:10 (NKJV)

For the Scripture says, "Whoever believes on Him will not be put to shame."

Romans 10:11 (NKJV)

For there is no distinction between Jew and Greek, for the same Lord over all is rich to all who call upon Him.

Romans 10:12 (NKJV)

For "whoever calls on the name of the Lord shall be saved."

Romans 10:13 (NKJV)

Faith

For by grace, you have been saved through faith, and that not of yourselves; it is the gift of God, not of works, lest anyone should boast.

Ephesians 2:8, 9 (NKJV)

Now faith is the substance of things hoped for, the evidence of things not seen.
By faith we understand that the worlds were framed by the Word of God, so that the things which are seen were not made of things which are visible.

Hebrews 11:1–3 (NKJV)

Without faith it is impossible to please Him, for he who comes to God must believe that He is, and that He is a rewarder of those who diligently seek Him.

Hebrews 11:6 (NKJV)

So, then faith comes by hearing, and hearing by the word of God.

Romans 10:17 (NKJV)

For we walk by faith, not by sight.

2 Corinthians 5:7 (NKJV)

Therefore, having been justified by faith, we have peace with God through our Lord Jesus Christ, through whom also we have access by faith into this grace in which we stand, and rejoice in hope of the glory of God.

Romans 5:1, 2 (NKJV)

For with God nothing will be impossible.

Luke 1:37 (NKJV)

I can do all things through [20]Christ who strengthens me.

Philippians 4:13 (NKJV)

...above all, taking the shield of faith with which you will be able to quench all the fiery darts of the wicked one. And take the helmet of salvation, and the sword of the Spirit, which is the word of God.

Ephesians 6:16, 17 (NKJV)

Genealogy of Jesus Christ, the Messiah

Genealogy of Jesus Christ, the Messiah

The book of the genealogy of Jesus Christ, the Son of David, the Son of Abraham: Abraham begot Isaac, Isaac begot Jacob, and Jacob begot Judah and his brothers. Judah begot Perez and Zerah by Tamar, Perez begot Hezron, and Hezron begot Ram. Ram begot Amminadab, Amminadab begot Nahshon, and Nahshon begot Salmon.

Matthew 1:1–4 (NKJV)

Salmon begot Boaz by Rahab, Boaz begot Obed by Ruth, Obed begot Jesse, and Jesse begot David the king. David the king begot Solomon by her [21]who had been the wife of Uriah. Solomon begot Rehoboam, Rehoboam begot Abijah, and Abijah begot Asa.

Matthew 1:5–7 (NKJV)

Asa begot Jehoshaphat, Jehoshaphat begot Joram, and Joram begot Uzziah. Uzziah begot Jotham, Jotham begot Ahaz, and Ahaz begot Hezekiah. Hezekiah begot Manasseh, Manasseh begot [22]Amon, and Amon begot Josiah. Josiah begot[23] Jeconiah and his brothers about the time they were carried away to Babylon.

Matthew 1:8–11 (NKJV)

And after they were brought to Babylon, Jeconiah begot Shealtiel, and Shealtiel begot Zerubbabel. Zerubbabel begot Abiud, Abiud begot Eliakim, and Eliakim begot Azor. Azor begot Zadok, Zadok begot Achim, and Achim begot Eliud. Eliud begot Eleazar, Eleazar begot Matthan, and Matthan begot Jacob.

Matthew 1:12–15 (NKJV)

And Jacob begot Joseph the husband of Mary, of whom was born Jesus who is called Christ. So, all the generations from Abraham to David are fourteen generations, from David until the captivity in Babylon are fourteen generations, and from the captivity in Babylon until Christ are fourteen generations.

Matthew 1:16, 17 (NKJV)

Transformation

Do not be conformed to this world, but be transformed by the renewing of your mind, that you may prove what is that good and acceptable and perfect will of God.

Romans 12:2 (NKJV)

Therefore, if anyone is in Christ, he is a new creation; old things have passed away; behold, all things have become new.

2 Corinthians 5:17 (NKJV)

So all of us who have had that veil removed can see and reflect the glory of the Lord. And the Lord—who is the Spirit—makes us more and more like him as we are changed into his glorious image.

2 Corinthians 3:18 (NLT)

Inheritance

All praise to God, the Father of our Lord Jesus Christ. It is by His great mercy that we have been born again, because God raised Jesus Christ from the dead.

Now we live with great expectation, and we have a priceless inheritance—an inheritance that is kept in heaven for you, pure and undefiled, beyond the reach of change and decay. And through your faith, God is protecting you by his power until you receive this salvation, which is ready to be revealed on the last day for all to see.

1 Peter 1:3–5 (NLT)

So be truly glad. There is wonderful joy ahead, even though you must endure many trials for a little while. These trials will show that your faith is genuine. It is being tested as fire tests and purifies gold—though your faith is far more precious than mere gold. So, when your faith remains strong through many trials, it will bring you much praise and glory and honor on the day when Jesus Christ is revealed to the whole world. You love him even though you have never seen him. Though you do not see him now, you trust him; and you rejoice with a glorious, inexpressible joy. The reward for trusting him will be the salvation of your souls.

1 Peter 1:6–9 (NLT)

For we ourselves were also once foolish, disobedient, deceived, serving various lust and pleasures, living in malice and envy, hateful and hating one another.

Titus 3:3 (NKJV)

But when the kindness and the love of God our Savior toward man appeared, not by works of righteousness which we have done, but according to His mercy He saved us, through the washing of regeneration and renewing of the Holy Spirit, whom He poured out on us abundantly through Jesus Christ our Savior, that having been justified by His grace we should become heirs according to the hope of eternal life.

Titus 3:4–7 (NKJV)

In Him also we have obtained an inheritance, being predestined according to the purpose of Him who works all things according to the counsel of His will, that we who first trusted in Christ should be to the praise of His glory. In Him you also trusted, after you heard the word of truth, the gospel of your salvation; in whom also, having believed, you were sealed with the Holy Spirit of promise, who is the guarantee of our inheritance until the redemption of the purchased possession, to the praise of His glory.

Ephesians 1:11–14 (NKJV)

For the Lord will not [24]cast off His people, Nor will He forsake His inheritance.

Psalm 94:14 (NKJV)

And whatever you do, do it heartily, as to the Lord and not to men, knowing that from the Lord you will receive the reward of the inheritance; for[25] you serve the Lord Christ.

Colossians 3:23, 24 (NKJV)

Relationship with God

Beloved, let us love one another, for love is of God; and everyone who loves is born of God and knows God. He who does not love does not know God, for God is love. In this the love of God was manifested toward us, that God has sent His only begotten Son into the world, that we might live through Him. In this is love, not that we loved God, but that He loved us and sent His Son to be the propitiation for our sins. Beloved, if God so loved us, we also ought to love one another.

1 John 4:7–11 (NKJV)

Therefore, know that the Lord your God, He is God, the faithful God who keeps covenant and mercy for a thousand generations with those who love Him and keep His commandments; and He repays those who hate Him to their face, to destroy them . . . He will repay him to his face.

Deuteronomy 7:9, 10 (NKJV)

And we have known and believed the love that God has for us. God is love, and he who abides in love abides in God, and God in him.

1 John 4:16 (NKJV)

Love suffers long and is kind; love does not envy; love does not parade itself, is not 26puffed up; does not behave rudely, does not seek its own, is not provoked, 27thinks no evil; does not rejoice in iniquity, but rejoices in the truth; bears all things, believes all things, hopes all things, endures all things.

1 Corinthians 13:4–7 (NKJV)

61

And now abide faith, hope, love, these three; but the greatest of these is love.

1 Corinthians 13:13 (NKJV)

Search for the Lord and for his strength; continually seek Him.

1 Chronicles 16:11 (NLT)

But above all these things put on love, which is the bond of perfection. And let the peace of God rule in your hearts, to which also you were called in one body; and be thankful.

Colossians 3:14, 15 (NKJV)

As many as received Him, to them He gave the [28]*right to become children of God, to those who believe in His name: who were born, not of blood, nor of the will of the flesh, nor of the will of man, but of God.*

John 1:12, 13 (NKJV)

...keep yourselves in the love of God, looking for the mercy of our Lord Jesus Christ unto eternal life.

Jude 1:21 (NKJV)

For I know the thoughts that I think towards you, says the Lord, thoughts of peace and not of evil, to give you a future and a hope. Then you will call upon Me and go pray to Me, and I will listen to you...I will be found by you, says the Lord.

Jeremiah 29:11–14 (NKJV)

Godliness and Eternal Life

The Father loves the Son, and has given all things into His hand. He who believes in the Son has everlasting life; and he who does not believe the Son shall not see life, but the wrath of God abides on him.

John 3:35, 36 (NKJV)

For the wages of sin is death, but the [29]gift of God is eternal life in Christ Jesus our Lord.

Romans 6:23 (NKJV)

Do not be deceived, God is not mocked; for whatever a man sows, that he will also reap. For he who sows to his flesh will of the flesh reap corruption, but he who sows to the Spirit will of the Spirit reap everlasting life.

Galatians 6:7, 8 (NKJV)

Jesus said to him, "I am the way, the truth, and the life. No one comes to the Father except through Me."

John 14:6 (NKJV)

...but whoever drinks of the water that I shall give him will never thirst. But the water I shall give him will become in him a fountain of water springing up into everlasting life.

John 4:14 (NKJV)

Most assuredly, I say to you, he who hears My word and believes in Him who sent Me has everlasting life, and shall not come into judgment, but has passed from death into life.

John 5:24 (NKJV)

My sheep hear My voice, and I know them, and they follow Me. And I give them eternal life, and they shall never perish; neither shall anyone snatch them out of my hand. My Father, who has given them to Me, is greater than all; and no one is able to snatch them out of My Father's hand. I and My Father are one.

John 10:27–30 (NKJV)

These things I have written to you who believe in the name of the Son of God, that you may know that you have eternal life, [30]and that you may continue to believe in the name of the Son of God.

1 John 5:13 (NKJV)

In all your ways acknowledge Him,
And He shall [31]direct your paths.

Proverbs 3:6 (NKJV)

This is the will of the Father who sent Me, that of all He has given Me I should lose nothing, but should raise it up at the last day. And this is the will of Him who sent Me, that everyone who sees the Son and believes in Him may have everlasting life; and I will raise him up at the last day.

John 6:39, 40 (NKJV)

Sin and
Eternal Death

"For behold, the day is coming,
Burning like an oven,
And all the proud, yes all who do wickedly will
be stubble.
And the day which is coming shall burn them up,"
Says the Lord of hosts,
"That will leave them neither root nor branch."

Malachi 4:1 (NKJV)

...as Sodom and Gomorrah, and the cities around
them in a similar manner to these, having given
themselves over to sexual immorality and gone
after strange flesh, are set forth as an example,
suffering the [32]vengeance of eternal fire.

Jude 1:7 (NKJV)

These shall be punished with everlasting
destruction from the presence of the Lord and the
glory of His power.

2 Thessalonians 1:9 (NKJV)

"Behold, all souls are Mine;
The soul of the father
As well as the soul of the son is Mine;
The soul who sins shall die.

Ezekiel 18:4 (NKJV)

"There is no peace," says the Lord, "for the
wicked."

Isaiah 48:22 (NKJV)

Do not be deceived, God is not mocked; for
whatever a man sows, that he will also reap. For

he who sows to his flesh reap corruption, but he who sows to the Spirit will of the Spirit reap everlasting life.

Galatians 6:7, 8 (NKJV)

So it will be at the end of the age. The angels will come forth, separate the wicked from among the just, and cast them into the furnace of fire. There will be wailing and gnashing of teeth.

Matthew 13:49, 50 (NKJV)

The Lord is not slack concerning His promise, as some count slackness, but is longsuffering toward [33]us, not willing that any should perish but that all should come to repentance. But the day of the Lord will come as a thief in the night, in which the heavens will pass away with a great noise, and the elements will melt with fervent heat; both the earth and the works that are in it will be [34]burned up.

2 Peter 3:9, 10 (NKJV)

For the wages of sin is death, but the gift of God is eternal life in Christ Jesus our Lord.

Romans 6:23 (NKJV)

There is salvation in no one else! God has given no other name under heaven by which we must be saved.

Acts 4:12 (NLT)

Satan

Satan

"How you are fallen from heaven,
O Lucifer, son of the morning![35]
How you are cut down to the ground,
You who weakened the nations!
For you have said in your heart:
'I will ascend into heaven,
I will exalt my throne above the stars of God;
I will also sit on the mount of the congregation
On the farthest sides of the north;
I will ascend above the heights of the clouds,
I will be like the Most High.'
Yet you shall be brought down to Sheol,
To the [36]*lowest depths of the Pit."*

Isaiah 14:12–15 (NKJV)

"...You were the seal of perfection,
Full of wisdom and perfect in beauty.
You were in Eden, the garden of God;
Every precious stone was your covering:
The sardius, topaz, and diamond,
Beryl, onyx, and jasper,
Sapphire, turquoise, and emerald with gold.
The workmanship of your timbrels and pipes
was prepared for you on the day you were created.

Ezekiel 28:12, 13 (NKJV)

"You were the anointed cherub who covers;
I established you;
You were on the holy mountain of God;
You walked back and forth in the midst of fiery
stones.
You were perfect in your ways from the day you
Were created,

73

Till iniquity was found in you.
"By the abundance of your trading
You became filled with violence within,
And you sinned;
Therefore I cast you as a profane thing
Out of the mountain of God;
And I destroyed you, O covering cherub,
From the midst of the fiery stones.

Ezekiel 28:14–16 (NKJV)

"Your heart was lifted up because of your beauty;
You corrupted your wisdom for the sake of your
splendor;
I cast you to the ground,
I laid you before kings,
That they might gaze at you.
"You defiled your sanctuaries
By the multitude of your iniquities,
By the iniquity of your trading;
Therefore, I brought fire from your midst;
It devoured you,
And I turned you to ashes upon the earth
In the sight of all who saw you.
All who knew you among the peoples are
astonished at
you;
You have become a horror,
And shall be no more forever."'"

Ezekiel 28:17–19 (NKJV)

Adam & Eve in the Garden of Eden

Now the serpent was more cunning than any beast of the field which the Lord God had made. And he said to the woman, "Has God indeed said, 'You shall not eat of every tree of the garden'?" And the woman said to the serpent, "We may eat the fruit of the trees of the garden; but of the fruit of the tree which is in the midst of the garden, God has said, 'You shall not eat it, nor shall you touch it, lest you die.'"

Genesis 3:1–3 (NKJV)

Then the serpent said to the woman, "You will not surely die. For God knows that in the day you eat of it your eyes will be opened, and you will be like God, knowing good and evil."
So, when the woman saw that the tree was good for food, that it was [37]pleasant to the eyes, and a tree desirable to make one wise, she took of its fruit and ate. She also gave to her husband with her, and he ate.

Genesis 3:4–6 (NKJV)

Then the eyes of both of them were open, and they knew that they were naked; and they sewed figs leaves together and made themselves [38]coverings.

Genesis 3:7 (NKJV)

And they heard the [39]sound of the Lord God walking in the garden in the [40]cool of the day, and Adam and his wife hid themselves from the presence of the Lord God among the trees of the garden.
Then the Lord God called to Adam and said to

him, "Where are you?"

So he said, "I heard Your voice in the garden, and I was afraid because I was naked; and I hid myself."

Genesis 3:8–10 (NKJV)

And He said, "Who told you that you were naked? Have you eaten from the tree of which I commanded you that you should not eat?"

Genesis 3:11 (NKJV)

Then the man said, "The woman whom You gave to be with me, she gave me of the tree, and I ate."
And the Lord God said to the woman, "What is this you have done?"
The woman said, "The serpent deceived me, and I ate."

Genesis 3:12, 13 (NKJV)

So, the Lord God said to the serpent:
"Because you have done this,
You are cursed more than all cattle,
And more than every beast of the field;
On your belly you shall go,
And you shall eat dust
All the days of your life.
And I will put enmity
Between you and the woman,
And between your seed and her Seed;
He shall bruise your head,
And you shall bruise His heel."

Genesis 3:14, 15 (NKJV)

Then He said to the woman,
"I will sharpen the pain of your pregnancy,
and in pain you will give birth.
And you will desire to control your husband,
but he will rule over you."
And to the man He said,
"Since you listened to your wife and ate from the
tree
whose fruit I commanded you not to eat,
the ground is cursed because of you.
All your life you will struggle to scratch a living
from it.

Genesis 3:16, 17 (NLT)

Both thorns and thistles it shall [41]bring forth for
you,
And you shall eat the herb of the field.
In the sweat of the face you shall eat bread
Till you return to the ground,
For out of it you were taken;
For dust you are,
And dust you shall return.

Genesis 3:18, 19 (NKJV)

And Adam called his wife's name Eve,[42] because
she was the mother of all living.
Also for Adam and his wife the Lord God made
tunics of skin, and clothed them.

Genesis 3:20, 21 (NKJV)

Then the Lord God said, "Behold, the man has
become like one of Us, to know good and evil. And
now, lest he put out his hand and take also of the

tree of life, and eat, and live forever"—therefore the Lord God sent him out of the garden of Eden to till the ground from which he was taken. So He drove out the man; and He placed cherubim at the east of the garden of Eden, and a flaming sword which turned every way, to guard the way to the tree of life.

Genesis 3:22–24 (NKJV)

Adam & The Creation of Eve

The Lord God said, "It is not good that man should be alone; I will make him a helper comparable to him." Out of the ground the Lord God formed every beast of the field and every bird of the air, and brought them to [43]Adam to see what he would call them. And whatever Adam called each living creature, that was its name.

Genesis 2:18, 19 (NKJV)

So Adam gave names to all cattle, to the birds of the air, and to every beast of the field. But for Adam there was not found a comparable to him.

Genesis 2:20 (NKJV)

And the Lord God caused a deep sleep to fall on Adam, and he slept; and He took one of his ribs, and closed up the flesh in its place. Then the rib which the Lord God had taken from man He [44]made into a woman, and He brought her to the man.

Genesis 2:21, 22 (NKJV)

And Adam said:
"This is now bone of my bones
And flesh of my flesh;
She shall be called [45]Woman,
Because she was taken out of [46]Man."
Therefore a man shall be[47] joined to his wife, and they shall become one flesh.
And they were both naked, the man and his wife, and were not ashamed.

Genesis 2:23–25 (NKJV)

Creation of
Adam

This is the history[48] of the heavens and the earth when they were created, in the day that the Lord God made the earth and the heavens, before any plant of the field was in the earth and before any herb of the field had grown. For the Lord God had not caused it to rain on the earth, and there was no man to till the ground; but a mist went up from the earth and watered the whole face of the ground. And the Lord God formed man of the dust of the ground, and breathed into his nostrils the breath of life; and man became a living being.

Genesis 2:4–7 (NKJV)

The Lord God planted a garden eastward in Eden, and there He put the man whom He had formed. And out of the ground the Lord God made every tree grow that is pleasant to the sight and good for food. The tree of life was also in the midst of the garden, and the tree of the knowledge of good and evil.

Now a river went out of Eden to water the garden, and from there it parted and became four river-heads. The name of the first is Pishon; it is the one which skirts the whole land of Havilah where there is gold. And the gold of that land is good. Bdellium and onyx stone are there. The name of the second river is Gihon; it is the one which goes around the whole land of Cush. The name of the third river is Hiddekel;[49] it is one which goes toward the east of Assyria.[50] The fourth is the Euphrates.

Genesis 2:8–14 (NKJV)

Creation of Adam

Then the Lord God took [51] the man put him in the garden of Eden to [52] tend and keep it. And the Lord God commanded the man, saying, "Of every tree of the garden you may freely eat; but of the tree of the knowledge of good and evil you shall not eat, for in the day that you eat of it you[53] shall surely die."

Genesis 2:15–17 (NKJV)

Out of the ground the Lord God formed every beast of the field and every bird of the air, and brought them to Adam to see what he would call them. And whatever Adam called each living creature, that was its name. So Adam gave names to all cattle, to the birds of the air, and to every beast of the field.

Genesis 2:19, 20 (NKJV)

Creation

Creation

In the beginning was the Word, and the Word was with God, and the Word was God. He was in the beginning with God. All things were made through Him, and without Him nothing was made that was made. In Him was life, and the life was the light of men. And the light shines in the darkness, and the darkness did not [54]comprehend it.

John 1:1–5 (NKJV)

For by Him all things were created that are in heaven and that are on earth, visible and invisible, whether thrones or dominions or [55]principalities or [56]powers. All things were created through Him and for Him. And He is before all things, and in Him all things consist. And He is the head of the body, the church, who is the beginning, the firstborn from the dead, that in all things He may have the preeminence.

Colossians 1:16–18 (NKJV)

By the Word of the Lord the heavens were made, And all the host of them by the breath of His mouth.

Psalm 33:6 (NKJV)

Before the mountains were brought forth, Or ever You [57]had formed the earth and the world, Even from everlasting to everlasting, You are God.

Psalm 90:2 (NKJV)

91

He has made the earth by His power,
He has established the world by His wisdom,
And has stretched out the heavens at His
discretion.

Jeremiah 10:12 (NKJV)

I have made the earth, the man and the beast that
are on the ground, by My great power and by My
outstretched arm, and have given it to whom it
seemed proper to Me.

Jeremiah 27:5 (NKJV)

I have made the earth,
And created man on it.
I—My hands—stretched out the heavens,
And all their host I have commanded.

Isaiah 45:12 (NKJV)

Then God said, "Let Us make man in Our image,
according to Our likeness; let them have dominion
over the fish of the sea, over the birds of the air,
and over the cattle, over [58]*all the earth and over*
every creeping thing that creeps on the earth."
So God created man in His own image; in the
image of God He created him; male and female
He created them.

Genesis 1:26, 27 (NKJV)

Then God blessed them, and God said to them, "Be fruitful and multiply; fill the earth and subdue it; have dominion over the fish of the sea, over the birds of the air, and over every living thing that [59]moves on the earth."

Genesis 1:28 (NKJV)

And God said, "See, I have given you every herb that yields seed which is on the face of all the earth, and every tree whose fruit yields seeds; to you it shall be for food. Also, to every beast of the earth, to every bird of the air, and to everything that creeps on the earth, in which there is [60]life, I have given every green herb for food"; and it was so. Then God saw everything that He had made, and indeed it was very good. So the evening and morning were the sixth day.

Genesis 1:29–31 (NKJV)

Thus the heavens and the earth, and all the host of them, were finished. And on the seventh day God ended His work which He had done, and He rested on the seventh day from all His work which He had done. Then God blessed the seventh day and sanctified it, because in it He rested from all His work which God had created and made.

Genesis 2:1–3 (NKJV)

The Blessing

The Blessing

"The Lord bless you and keep you;
The Lord make His face shine upon you,
And be gracious to you,
The Lord lift up His countenance upon you,
And give you peace."

Numbers 6:24–26 (NKJV)

ENDNOTES

1   1 Corinthians 6:20 Nestle-Aland Greek New Testament
    United Bible Societies (NU) omits the rest of v.20.

2   Ephesians 1:6 Literally *bestowed grace favor upon us*

3   Isaiah 55:11 *empty,* without fruit

4   Revelation 22:13 NU, M-Text (M) *First and the Last,
    the Beginning and the End*

5   Colossians 1:16 *rulers*

6   Colossians 1:16 *authorities*

7   Genesis 1:26 Syriac *all the wild animals of*

8   Psalm 82:6 Judges; Hebrew *Elohim,* Literally *mighty
    ones* or *gods*

9   1 Corinthians 15:47 *earthy*

10   1 Corinthians 15:47 NU omits *the Lord*

11   1 Corinthians 15:49 M *let us also bear*

12   Revelation 1:5 NU *loves us and freed;* M *loves us and
    washed*

13   Revelation 1:6 NU, M *a kingdom*

14   John 14:14 NU *ask Me*

15   Matthew 4:10 M *Get behind Me*

16   Romans 6:23 *free gift*

17 Matthew 4:17 *has drawn near*

18 Joel 2:32 Or *delivered*

19 Joel 2:32 Or *salvation*

20 Philippians 4:13 NU *Him who*

21 Matthew 1:6 Words in italic type have been added for clarity. They are not found in the original Greek.

22 Matthew 1:10 NU *Amos*

23 Matthew 1:11 Or *Coniah* or *Jehoiachin*

24 Psalm 94:14 *abandon*

25 Colossians 3:24 NU omits *for* John 1:12 *authority*

26 1 Corinthians 13:4 *arrogant*

27 1 Corinthians 13:5 *keeps no accounts of evil*

28 John 1:12 *authority*

29 Romans 6:23 *free gift*

30 1 John 5:13 NU omits the rest of verse 13.

31 Proverbs 3:6 Or *make smooth* or *straight*

32 Jude 1:7 *punishment*

33 2 Peter 3:9 NU *you*

34 2 Peter 3:10 NU *laid bare,* literally *found*

35 Isaiah 14:12 Literally *Day Star*

36 Isaiah 14:15 Literally *recesses*

37 Genesis 3:6 Literally *a desirable thing*

38 Genesis 3:7 *girding coverings*

39 Genesis 3:8 Or *voice*

40 Genesis 3:8 Or *wind, breeze*

41 Genesis 3:18 *cause to grow*

42 Genesis 3:20 Literally *Life* or *Living*

43 Genesis 2:19 Or *the man*

44 Genesis 2:22 Literally *built*

45 Genesis 2:23 Hebrew *Ishshah*

46 Genesis 2:23 Hebrew *Ish*

47 Genesis 2:24 Literally *cling*

48 Genesis 2:4 Hebrew *toledoth,* Literally *generations*

49 Genesis 2:14 Or *Tigris*

50 Genesis 2:14 Hebrew *Ashshur*

51 Genesis 2:15 Or *Adam*

52 Genesis 2:15 *cultivate*

53 Genesis 2:17 Literally *dying you shall die*

54 John 1:5 Or *overcome*

55 Colossians 1:16 *rulers*

56 Colossians 1:16 *authorities*

57 Psalm 90:2 Literally *gave birth to*

58 Genesis 1:26 Syriac *all the wild animals of*

59 Genesis 1:28 *moves about on*

60 Genesis 1:30 *a living soul*

CPSIA information can be obtained
at www.ICGtesting.com
Printed in the USA
LVHW042236300322
714844LV00012B/1675